CHRISTMAS IN THE COUNTRY

Books by Margery Darrell

The Rodgers and Hart Song Book,
Edited and with an Introduction by
Richard Rodgers, Foreword by Oscar
Hammerstein II, Text by
Margery Darrell, 1951.

*Once Upon A Time, The Fairy Tale
World of Arthur Rackham,*
by Margery Darrell, 1972.

CURRIER & IVES
Christmas in the Country

EDITED BY MARGERY DARRELL

THE PYNE PRESS

Princeton

The publishers wish to express their
indebtedness to the Museum of the City
of New York, and particularly to
Miss Charlotte LaRue, for kindly making
available to them the prints in this book,
which are a part of the Harry T. Peters
Collection. The editor also wishes
especially to thank Miss Elizabeth Roth,
Keeper of Prints of the Print Collection
of the New York Public Library;
Mrs. Thelma Gordon, Art Librarian
of the Westport, Conn., Public Library;
and Mrs. Grace Donaldson of the
Pequot Library, Southport, Conn.,
for their generous assistance and advice
in seeking out factual material to
accompany the lithographs.

CHRISTMAS IN THE COUNTRY

INTRODUCTION

The varying fortunes of Currier & Ives prints in the world of art could be treated at length, but they can also be described in a sentence. The main trouble, from an artistic point of view, is that they were just what their creators set out to make them: that is, popular. They were uncompromisingly middle-brow—even low-brow, upon occasion. Specifically designed to please people, they appeared at a time when, as one critic wrote, "Artistic standards caused no discrimination because there were none." The critic, incidentally, was Charles Messer Snow, antiques editor of the *New York Sun*, writing in 1933, and he liked Currier & Ives. In the second half of the nineteenth century, Americans were so occupied with wars, building railroads, sailing ships, settling the West, racing horses, experimenting with steamboats, panning for gold, and making money that they had no time to consider what they should or should not like in the way of art. In these conditions, Currier & Ives, who really didn't care either, flourished.

No claim has ever been advanced that the prints of Currier & Ives were great art. But, on the other hand, unless the viewer is opposed on principle to honest sentiment, he is bound to respond to some. No one has ever defended the aesthetic merits of the "sentimentals," as they are called, or the "comics," or many of the political cartoons such as *Honest Abe Taking Them on the Half Shell* (the "them" were Stephen Douglas and John Breckinridge). But the clipper ships of Charles Parsons, the prints of Arthur Fitzwilliam Tait, the winter scenes by George Henry Durrie, and the over six hundred horse prints (which by themselves constitute a whole history of the American standardbred horse in this country) have been generally admired for over a hundred years.

Harry T. Peters, the individualistic collector who more than anyone else was responsible for the reassessment of the prints in the twenties, observed in 1942 that it had taken less time to accomplish a Currier & Ives revival than most others. By the time the firm had closed its door in 1907, it was within twenty years of being rediscovered. But even Peters remarked that "Judged purely as art, little of the work of Currier & Ives would have lived." "Nevertheless," he went on, "as a well-rounded, comprehensive, and truly representative picture of an age, all of it has lived and will live." And, it should be added, many of the big prints, which sold for three or four dollars and are known as the large folios, are quite able to hold their own by today's standards. The bulk of the Currier & Ives output, of course, was more modest.

The Currier & Ives period, which spanned seventy-two years, was the era in which it is often said that the United States came of age, and no phase of this development was neglected by these "Printmakers to the American People." A sales letter from the 1870s announced that the firm had eleven hundred subjects to choose from. It went on to list the biggest sellers: "The Catalogue comprises Juvenile, Domestic, Love Scenes, Kittens and Puppies, Ladies' Heads, Catholic Religious, Patriotic, Landscapes, Vessels, Comic, School Rewards and Drawing Studies, Flowers and Fruits, Motto Cards, Horses, Family Registers, Memory Pieces and Miscellaneous, in Great Variety, and all Elegant and Salable Pictures." Lumped unceremoniously under "Miscellaneous" were some of the most distinguished prints, which appealed less to the mass market—the country and pioneer home scenes, historical events, portraits (which were a who's-who of mid-century America), Mississippi River prints, railroad prints, whaling scenes, city views and sites, wild game studies, and hunting and fishing scenes, all of which are among the most valuable prints today.

The firm was nothing if not broad-minded and democratic in its choice of subjects. They ranged from the heroic *Surrender of Cornwallis* to *P. T. Barnum's Bearded Lady*. They included *Jesus Falls for the Second Time (on Calvary)*, *The Age of Brass or The Triumph of Women's Rights*, and *Holidays in the Country: Troublesome Flies*. But throughout their career, Currier & Ives were undeniably wholesome. A lithograph of *Washington Taking Leave of the Officers of His Army*, which showed him with a wine glass raised gracefully aloft, was later redrawn to eliminate the wine glass. In the revised version, his hand was raised gracefully aloft, around nothing. In another instance James Ives instructed an artist to remove a drunken Indian from one of the comic series, not at all because he was an Indian maligned, but because the firm of Currier & Ives stood strong for temperance. The comic prints, in which the greatest lapses of taste—by today's standards—could and did appear (their attitude toward blacks reflected all the prejudice of the period, even in the North) were described in the catalogue thus: "The effect of these Comic Pictures is to drive away the blues and promise hearty and wholesome laughter. They are just the thing to make a room bright and cheerful and everybody who enters it good-natured and lively." Whatever it might show, a Currier & Ives print was nothing you ever had to hide from the family.

The history of Currier & Ives began with Nathaniel Currier, who was born in Roxbury, Massachusetts, in 1813. At fifteen he went to work for the firm of William S. & John Pendleton in Boston, the first establishment to successfully use the new technique of lithography which had recently been invented in Bavaria by Alois Senefelder. The process was not complicated, but it was tricky. It allowed for very few second thoughts on the part of the lithographer. A porous stone was finely ground, by hand, using sand and a grindstone, so that it had "tooth" and would absorb ink. An artist, using a grease crayon which repelled ink, drew a design on the stone. The stone was inked, and the print was pulled. (The ink later used by Currier & Ives, according to Harry T. Peters, was their own formula: a compound of beef suet, goose grease, white wax, castile soap, gum mastic, shellac, and gas black. The crayons used, originally imported from France, were developed by Nathaniel Currier's brother, Charles, and Fanny Palmer, a house artist, and were found to be better than the imported ones.)

If when drawing on the stone, the artist wanted to erase a line, that could be done, but he could not effectively put another line in its place because the grain of the stone was lost. Lithographers, making the transfer to stone from a painting or drawing could, of course, make revisions of their own, and in the hurly-burly of the Currier & Ives operation, they often did. So the lithographer was often as important as the original artist. Louis Maurer, who with Fanny Palmer was the only regular artist on the payroll, once transferred a Thomas Worth horse drawing to stone, a print entitled A *Disputed Heat*. He left out the middle of the drawing, however, telling Ives he thought the print needed central figures to pull it together. Ives agreed. A trio of embattled horsemen was inserted, and the print was approved. Lithographers in other firms took similar liberties with their assignments.

Nathaniel Currier left Pendleton and went to New York by way of Philadelphia in 1834 where he set up a business at 1 Wall Street. His first great success was a print showing the fire on the steamboat *Lexington*, an ill-fated vessel that went down off Stonington, Connecticut, with one hundred forty souls aboard. All but a handful were lost in the icy waters or burned to death. Currier's print, which appeared three days after the disaster, was the equivalent of a newspaper extra, in a day when there were none. It was picked up by the *New York Sun* and hawked on the street, making Currier a celebrity overnight. This print, and a few others such as the *Ruins of the Merchants' Exchange, New York, after the Destructive Conflagration of Dec. 16 & 17, 1835*, established Nathaniel Currier as the founder of a new pictorial medium similar to the tabloids or the picture magazines of our own day.

Although chromolithography was developed by the time Currier's firm reached its greatest success, neither he nor Ives ever explored its possibilities. Coloring was always done by hand, either in the factory at 33 Spruce Street in Manhattan or, in the case of the more ambitious large folio prints, by outside artists, often on their uppers, who were paid one cent apiece for the small prints, and one dollar for twelve of the large folios. This meant that there was often a considerable variety of coloring schemes for a single picture. If a print sold better than expected and had to be rushed back into production, the later versions might be quite different from the original. Moreover—may the collector beware—Currier & Ives prints were often sold uncolored. Many prints for sale today are not the work of the dozen or so girls who worked in the factory under the guidance of James Ives and had much to say about the proper shade of vermillion for Lincoln's bier (brilliant) or the blue of the sky in San Francisco (blinding). They may be the work of a mid-century schoolgirl.

In the years of the firm's greatest eminence, its offices on Nassau Street became a meeting-place for celebrities of the day. When Horace Greeley (himself the editor of the New York *Tribune*), or P. T. Barnum or Henry Ward Beecher wanted to know what was going on, they went down to the shop to find out. There Currier or Ives might hit upon a hot idea for a print and assign it on the spot. Or an artist with a sketch might bring it in on speculation. In any case, Currier & Ives bought the art work outright, often for as little as five dollars. What they did with it, how they altered it, or how they sold it, was up to them. There were no such things as royalties or residual rights.

Copyright laws in that era were largely honored in the breach. Currier & Ives were pirated by other lithographers who often copied a print exactly, changing only the company name. And Currier & Ives, too, sometimes adopted foreign prints with the same fine disregard for credits. Louis Maurer did a series based on a British set of Shakespeare's *A Midsummer Night's Dream*.

Nathaniel Currier took his brother, Charles, into his business, and Charles in turn introduced him to James Merritt Ives, who had married his wife's sister. In 1852 Ives began work in the firm as a bookkeeper; in five years he was made a partner. Thomas Worth later said that early after Ives's arrival he found it necessary to sell an idea to both the partners, not just Currier. Ives was the gregarious sporting one; Currier was gracious, always polite, and more reserved. Ives accompanied Worth to the race track where Worth "got" the horses from life. And it was Ives who supervised many of the artists with a self-taught talent of his own. He often added human figures to other artists' backgrounds, corrected the coloring and wrote the voluminous captions. One of his most fulsome creations read: "*Imported Messenger* The Great Fountain Head—in America—of 'The Messenger Blood', Foaled 1780, got by Mambrino, he by Engineer, he by Sampson, he by Blaze, he by Flying Childers, he by the famous Darley Arabian. Messenger's Dam was by Turf, he by Matchem, he by Cade, he by the great Godolphin Arabian, and the sire of the Dam of Messenger's Dam was also by the Godolphin Arabian." As it could be quickly seen, Ives was interested in horses.

Jolly fellow though he was, Ives had his dignity to think of. Once Worth overstepped himself, presenting Ives with a drawing entitled *Mr. Ives, of Currier & Ives Print Service, at the Race Track in Hartford, Had His Hat Taken Off by the Celebrated Black Trotter "Judge Fullerton", One of the Most Vicious Beasts of all Time*. The drawing never again saw the light of day.

In all the years of the company's existence, from seven to eight thousand prints were issued, many of which have now disappeared. They were sold in a number of ways: by mail, by agents as distant as London or the Continent, in the retail shop on Spruce Street, and by peddlers on the road, who usually carried the small or medium sizes because they were easier to handle. (Some of the large folios measure up to twenty-eight by forty inches.) A particular effort was made to reach certain outlets which were sure to give the prints the maximum visibility: "Dealers in Carriages, Harness and Horse Furniture, Guns, Fishing Tackle and Sporting Goods, will find them a great attraction for their windows, while for Bar-Rooms, Saloons, Hotels, and Stable Offices, they are absolutely indispensable." No print-maker today goes seeking this market.

The phenomenal success of the firm was due to several factors, and the management of the two partners was a large part of it. But it was also due to the fact that Currier & Ives prints filled a public need not being met by any other source. They supplied the American people with a kind of picture journalism, in color. Their only competitors were the pictures in *Harper's Weekly* or *Frank Leslie's Illustrated Paper,* which were all black and white. When photography reached the point where it could serve the same purpose, and more quickly after the event, the handwriting was on the wall for Currier & Ives. Currier retired after forty-six years in 1880. Ives, who was eleven years his junior and young enough to have fought in the Civil War, worked until 1895. Both men turned their interests over to their sons, but neither son had the talent nor the opportunity their fathers had enjoyed. In 1902 Edward Currier sold out to Chauncey Ives, and Ives in turn made way for the son of the former sales manager, Daniel Logan, Jr. Logan was unable to carry on because of illness, and in 1907 the business was liquidated. The only person who had the foresight to collect anything like a complete set of Currier & Ives prints (up to 1880) was Nathaniel's brother, Charles. But he collected them in a damp Brooklyn basement, and when the crates were opened after his death, most of the prints were beyond saving.

Fortunately, other people who loved them saved them. But it took some time for their charm and historical value to be recognized and acknowledged. In the twenties, when Harry T. Peters began to put together his pioneer collection, he encountered considerable ridicule. A fellow print buff, visiting Peters at his house one day, admired a set of English prints and then remarked, "Once you get sense enough to burn and get rid of all the Currier & Ives junk, you will become a collector." The same man, when reminded some years later of the conversation, admitted, "Well, you're not as big a fool as I thought you were."

The established art world was just as intolerant. About 1920 a group of art critics organized an exhibition in New York of American bad taste, in which Currier & Ives were prominent. At the first auction sale of Currier & Ives prints in 1921, collectors scoffed at the "crudities," as they called them. Peters, whose social and business credentials were impeccable (he was Master of the Hounds at the Meadowbrook Hunt Club in Long Island) was described in the September 1931 issue of *Prints* as "formerly a coal dealer . . . who has developed into a very good historian in this field." And Winfred Porter Truesdell, editor of *The Print Connoisseur* had some biting words to say about the "portraits of aenemic females labelled Agnes, Lucy and Adelaide," which were the backbone of the Currier & Ives business.

By 1952, however, the fortunes of the firm had come full circle. The Metropolitan Museum of Art in New York graciously accepted its first gift of Currier & Ives prints and promptly put them on display. Scholars hastened to reassess them and historians hailed them, as if they had never seen them before, for what they unquestionably were: an invaluable and unique record of life in nineteenth century America. Currier and Ives, whose simple aim had been to provide value for money, achieved a fame far more lasting than their more celebrated and self-important contemporaries. Today, nearly a hundred and fifty years later, in an America they would find almost unrecognizable, the two men still fulfil their original purpose: "To Provide Colored Engravings for the People . . . Pleasant and Humorous Designs Free from Coarseness and Vulgarity . . . Prints that have become a Staple Article and which are in Great Demand in Every Part of the Country."

Twelve of their "Pleasant Designs" are collected in this book. Blazing yule logs and stockings hung by the chimney with care are missing; interior scenes (except for death-beds) were generally ignored by Currier & Ives, in spite of the vast range of their subjects. Their American Christmas lay in the majesty of the great white world outside and the rugged pleasures of the pioneer. For him in an ebullient period of expansion and energy, work and play were virtually synonymous. The daily chores in a snowy farm-yard, the carefree hour at the skating pond, the holiday glee of a schoolboy bringing home a Christmas tree, the conviviality of the ice-cutters or the ice-sailors or the farmers racing their trotters home from church: this was the Christmas world of Currier & Ives.

Margery Darrell
Owenoke,
Westport, Connecticut
June 3, 1974

CHRISTMAS SNOW

What a great change does a fall of snow produce on the face of the landscape! A fine, bright morning perchance follows, and the eye fairly aches, while looking upon the glittering prospect which lies around. Hill, and wood, and field, and footpath, the long highway, are mantled over with snow, upon which the wagon moves along with scarce a sound, and the horse is beside you before you are aware of it; for every noise is deadened by the deep fall of snow. That is not a morning to sit moping over the fire, when so much amusement is to be found out of doors—when there are fortifications to erect, and houses to build, and snow-men to make, and a snow-ball to roll along, until it is as high as our own heads; and, above all, a good-natured snow-balling match to take place between two parties of boys, where we are sure neither to injure ourselves, nor do any one harm. That is a morning to tie a thick comforter round the neck, lace the boots tightly, and put on the stoutest pair of worsted gloves, and sally out in the keen, cold, bracing air, knee-deep among the clean, white untrodden snow; for the sky is blue overhead, and the sun shines bright, and he only, who cares not to come home with a pair of rosy cheeks, will sit and keep company with the cat by the fireside.

The Boys' Winter Book by Thomas Miller, 1847

CHRISTMAS SNOW
1872-1874

Currier & Ives prints were issued in four sizes, described today as large, medium, small and very small. This one, which measures 7.15 by 4.15 inches, is the smallest size and undated as well as unsigned. (Its approximate date, however, has been determined by collectors using the address in the lower right hand corner, which was a Currier & Ives establishment during the seventies.) But modest as it is, *Christmas Snow* shows much of the vigor and honest homeliness of its creators' more ambitious works. Three small boys are shown uprooting Christmas trees; whether the building in the left background is a cottage with a wood-pile, as it is usually described in Currier & Ives literature, or a shop where the boys can sell the wood for kindling is for the reader to decide. Currently valued at about $200, the print probably sold originally for about twenty cents on a table outside the retail store in New York City, or to peddlers for a wholesale rate. A peddler could call at the store in the morning, stock up on the latest releases, and return his unsold wares for cash at the end of the day. Currier & Ives dealt strictly in cash, with everybody.

PUBLISHED BY CURRIER & IVES   125 NASSAU ST. NEW YORK

CHRISTMAS SNOW.

THE SNOW-STORM

Announced by all the trumpets of the sky,
Arrives the snow, and, driving o'er the fields,
Seems nowhere to alight; the whited air
Hides hills and woods, the river, and the heaven,
And veils the farm-house at the garden's end.
The sled and traveller stopped, the courier's feet
Delayed, all friends shut out, the housemates sit
Around the radiant fireplace, enclosed
In a tumultuous privacy of storm.
      Come see the north wind's masonry.
Out of an unseen quarry evermore
Furnished with tile, the fierce artificer
Curves his white bastions with projected roof
Round every windward stake, or tree or door.
Speeding, the myriad-handed, his wild work
So fanciful, so savage, nought cares he
For number or proportion. Mockingly,
On coop or kennel he hangs Parian wreaths;
   A swanlike form invests the hidden thorn;
Fills up the farmer's lane from wall to wall,
Maugre the farmer's sighs; and at the gate
A tapering turret overtops the work.
And when his hours are numbered, and the world
Is all his own, retiring, as he were not,
Leaves, when the sun appears, astonished Art
To mimic in slow structures, stone by stone,
Built in an age, the mad wind's night-work,
The frolic architecture of the snow.

The Snow-Storm by Ralph Waldo Emerson, 1841

THE SNOW-STORM
undated

Snow storms were a favorite subject for romantic nineteenth-century writers such as William Cullen Bryant, John Greenleaf Whittier, Emerson, and Thoreau, and the popular art of the day reflected the same preoccupation with nature, especially in its more awesome and majestic forms. (Whittier, whose long poem "Snow-Bound, A Winter Idyll" is probably the most famous of American winter poems, was a good friend of Nathaniel Currier's and a frequent guest at Currier's country home in Amesbury, Massachusetts.) Located in New York City for seventy-three years, Currier & Ives displayed a strong Yankee bias in their prints. Typical scenes were New England or Western in character, seldom Southern. During the Civil War the firm made no secret of its loyalties, although in a Presidential election they sometimes soft-pedalled their sympathies. They went so far, occasionally, as to publish a print under another name, such as a "Peter Smith" of "2 Spruce Street" used on a lithograph entitled *The Presidential Fishing Party of 1848*. (Since 2 Spruce Street was then occupied by Nathaniel Currier, it seems clearly to be his.) *The Snow-Storm* is a typical Currier & Ives Northern scene, undated and unsigned like much of their work and probably the product of many hands.

THE SNOW-STORM.

NEW YORK, PUBLISHED BY CURRIER & IVES, 152 NASSAU ST.

ICE-BOAT RACE
ON THE HUDSON

There is probably no other sport which combines such an amount of excitement and exhilaration as ice-yachting. The danger, the tremendous pace, causing a nervous excitement; the ringing sound of the steel runners as they fly over the ice, and the very frailness of the vessel, combine to produce a series of impressions which must be experienced to be appreciated. As the yacht glides along over the glassy surface of the Hudson . . . suddenly, an express train is seen dashing its way along the banks of the opposite shore. At once the helm is turned, and the vessel bounds forward eager for the race. In a moment or two the yacht is alongside the train, the engineer salutes and pulls the throttle of his iron steed wide open, the passengers wave their handkerchiefs, the challenge is accepted, the helmsman puts the yacht about, and the race is begun. The wind along the shore is puffy and changeable, and for a moment the train seems to be leaving us behind; but, as we round a bend in the river the full force of the wind is felt once more, and the yacht dashes ahead of the train, now teeming with excited passengers, as if the engineer were running at half-speed instead of at his greatest. Still another moment and the train is hidden from view by an intervening cliff and tunnel, and when the smoke of the engine is observed again, the ice-yacht is too far ahead to give even the semblance of a contest to what promised to be an exciting and close race. The yacht is eased and drops back again alongside the train, the engineer salutes his conqueror with three shrill whistles, and another race is begun, only to end as before.

Spirit of the Times by Henry A. Buck

ICE-BOAT RACE
ON THE HUDSON
1872-1874

The sport of ice-sailing was not invented in the United States, but it was most highly developed here. (Ice-boats had been used for centuries in Finland and on the canals of Holland, for transport.) The first ice yacht club was found in Poughkeepsie in 1861; a few years later such redoubtable social figures as John A. Roosevelt, Archibald Rogers, and Colonel E. Harrison Sanford organized the Hudson River Ice Yacht Club, which set the tone and ground rules for ice-boat racing. Roosevelt owned the largest yacht built, a sloop measuring sixty-eight feet long spreading 1,007 square feet of canvas. Rogers owned the *Jack Frost* with 911, and others owned yachts with cat rigs, ranging from 600 to 900 square feet in sail area. After some experimentation (members often built a boat a year) it was found that about fifty feet was the optimal length with a proportionate spread of sail. The construction of the racers was simple: a triangular framework of timber, mounted on three steel runners, the after one of which moved horizontally, acting as a rudder. Even on the Hudson the racing season was short, no more than thirty days and sometimes only six when conditions were right. It was, however, a heady if expensive sport: the speed record for an ice-yacht was set by Colonel Sanford, with qualified timekeepers, at seventy-two miles per hour. At this rate, it could easily outdistance a train, or for that matter, any conveyance of the day.

ICE-BOAT RACE ON THE HUDSON.

"TROTTING CRACKS"
ON THE SNOW

Their carriages of every kind are very unlike ours; those belonging to private individuals seem all constructed with a view to summer use, for which they are extremely well calculated, but they are by no means comfortable in winter. The stage-coaches are heavier and much less comfortable than those of France; to those of England they can bear no comparison. I never saw any harness that I could call handsome, nor any equipage which, as to horses, carriage, harness, and servants, could be considered as complete. The sleighs are delightful, and constructed at so little expense that I wonder we have not all got them in England, lying by in waiting for the snow, which often remains with us long enough to permit their use. Sleighing is much more generally enjoyed by night than by day, for what reason I could never discover, unless it be, that no gentlemen are to be found disengaged from business in the mornings. Nothing, certainly, can be more agreeable than the gliding smoothly and rapidly along, deep sunk in soft furs, the moon shining with almost mid-day splendour, the air of crystal brightness, and the snow sparkling on every side, as if it were sprinkled with diamonds. And then the noiseless movement of the horses, so mysterious and unwonted, and the gentle tinkling of the bells you meet and carry, all help at once to soothe and excite the spirits.

Domestic Manners of the Americans by Mrs. Frances Trollope, 1832

"TROTTING CRACKS"
ON THE SNOW
1858

One of the most exciting holiday diversions was racing trotters on the snow. Every family of any means had at least one horse (for two centuries in this country all freight, passengers, farm equipment, and mail moved by horse-power), and the family horse was a major investment. In 1820 he cost about a hundred dollars. If he was not only serviceable but fast, the owner had a lot of fun as well as a good buy. Trotters, with their distinctive diagonal gait, provide the least comfortable of rides under saddle (an English saying of the period went, "A butcher rides a trotter"), but for the same reason they have greater balance with a wagon, sulky, carriage or sleigh. Putting their feet down diagonally instead of laterally like a pacer or in rotary fashion like many other running animals, they are steady and strong. This celebrated lithograph shows eleven of the crack trotters of the day with the most famous of them, Flora Temple, prominently placed in the middle. Little Flora Temple, a dainty undersized mare, was a particular favorite with the ladies who admired her grace, and with the gentlemen who quite simply liked her speed. Her record for the mile, upon her retirement at sixteen, was a revolutionary 2:21. At one time or another she had bested almost all comers, including Lancer and Prince, also shown here. This print by Louis Maurer shows the horses with all four feet off the ground at once, a rather unlikely circumstance since a trotter at full tilt is in this position only a quarter of the time. But it does demonstrate the thoroughness of Maurer's horse lore, since it was not until Leland Stanford commissioned a photographic study some twenty years later that it was established that trotters, unlike horses with other gaits, actually do run this way. On the other hand, Maurer may have drawn them all this way to show the maximum of action. With all respect to Maurer, whose taste and talent were indisputably first rate, no Currier & Ives artist could afford to ignore the demands of a good picture.

"TROTTING CRACKS" ON THE SNOW.

WINTER PASTIME

Oh! what skating there was in those days! Some could cut out their names upon the ice; others make all kinds of picturesque flourishes; and not a few, the moment their skates were fixed on, after much trouble, showed the ice their heels, and came down with a loud bump, which caused all the bystanders to laugh again. These some good-natured skaters would occasionally take in tow, by bidding them lay hold of the end of their hook-stick, while they went foremost, and thus they were dragged along; and so, after a little practice, and a few more falls, they were enabled to take care of themselves, and, in a few hours, make a stroke or two much to their own satisfaction. . . . But sliding was much the liveliest amusement of all. You never saw such slides as we were wont to have upon the river, when it was frozen over; for we cared but little about them unless they were at least twenty yards long. Then we had one up, and another down; and we were ever upon each other's heels: for if one boy halted a moment, another was sure to shout out, 'Keep the pot a-boiling!' . . . And then, there were some boys who could go the whole length upon one leg; and others who glided along with both their feet together; some who slided with the left leg first, and others with the right; and many so clever, that they could turn themselves round, with their faces to those who followed; and we would lay hold of one another, and shoot off when halfway down; and do a many more other things, which would set a town-bred boy a-wondering.

The Boys' Winter Book by Thomas Miller, 1847

WINTER PASTIME
1855

Currier & Ives produced two prints with this title, this one in 1855 by Fanny Palmer and another in 1870, unsigned. Both show skating scenes and are worth about five hundred dollars today. Fanny Palmer was a frail, sad-eyed lady of gentle British birth who went to work to support a husband and a son in a day when ladies stayed home. Her husband, a handsome fellow whom she often used as a model in her hunting scenes, was also given to drink. He fell downstairs one day and broke his neck, prompting James Ives to remark, according to one account, that it was "the best thing he ever did." Her son, who took after him, died at the age of 33 of pneumonia. Fanny Palmer, meanwhile, became one of the most versatile and important figures in the Currier & Ives firm, remaining there until her death in 1876 at the age of 64. She specialized in backgrounds and was often driven to Long Island in Nathaniel Currier's buggy to sketch rural scenery. Sometimes figures were then inserted by other artists such as Otto Knirsch or Louis Maurer. But she also produced many famous lithographs which were entirely her own, such as the one at right. It was she, too, who often provided the model for the phalanx of girls who were the staff colorists, and she worked closely with Charles Currier in developing his lithographic crayons, which were acknowledged to be the best available. Unlike many artists, she was capable of drawing directly on stone, and she served as lithographer for the work of many other artists, usually without a credit.

Entered according to Act of Congress in the year 1855, by N. Currier, in the Clerk's Office of the District Court of the Southern District of New York.

WINTER PASTIME.

WINTER SPORTS –
PICKEREL FISHING

Early in the morning, while all things are crisp with frost, men come with fishing-reels and slender lunch, and let down their fine lines through the snowy field to take pickerel and perch; wild men, who instinctively follow other fashions and trust other authorities than their townsmen, and by their goings and comings stitch towns together in parts where else they would be ripped. They sit and eat their luncheon in stout fear-naughts on the dry oak leaves on the shore, as wise in natural lore as the citizen is in artificial. They never consult with books, and know and can tell much less than they have done. The things which they practice are said not yet to be known. Here is one fishing for pickerel with grown perch for bait. You look into his pail with wonder as into a summer pond, as if he kept summer locked up at home, or knew where she had retreated. How, pray, did he get these in midwinter? Oh, he got worms out of rotten logs since the ground froze, and so he caught them. His life itself passes deeper in nature than the studies of the naturalist penetrate; himself a subject for the naturalist. The latter raises the moss and bark gently with his knife in search of insects; the former lays open logs to their core with his axe, and moss and bark fly far and wide. He gets his living by barking trees. Such a man has some right to fish, and I love to see nature carried out in him. The perch swallows the grub-worm, the pickerel swallows the perch, and the fisherman swallows the pickerel; and so all the chinks in the scale of being are filled.

Walden by Henry David Thoreau, 1854

WINTER SPORTS—
PICKEREL FISHING
1872

This unsigned lithograph is from Currier & Ives's famous group of sporting prints. In general, unsigned prints are of less value than signed ones, but the sporting prints have always been one of the most popular and valuable categories. Nathaniel Currier, who was nothing if not a merchandiser, advertised his prints in mailing pieces which broke down his inventory into subject groups. He also made a point of producing sets of pictures, so that if a buyer bought one, he might be persuaded to buy them all. A companion piece to the one at right, although in a more sophisticated style, is Arthur Fitzwilliam Tait's *American Winter Sports—Trout Fishing on Chateaugay Lake*. The single most famous Currier & Ives in this group (or in any other) is *The Life of a Hunter—A Tight Fix*, also by Tait, which shows a hunter under attack by a grizzly bear. It brought $7500 at a recent auction, the record price for a Currier & Ives lithograph to date. The sportsmen at right, while not so rustic as those in the preceding quotation from Thoreau, are using a primitive technique described by him in a later passage of *Walden*. The fisherman places branches over his hole in the ice, fastens the end of his line to a stick to prevent its being pulled through, runs the slack line over a twig of the branch and ties a leaf to it. Thus he can loll on the shore or skate on the lake with an eye on the branch. When the leaf goes down, he has a bite.

Published by Currier & Ives

Entered according to act of Congress in the year 1872, by Currier & Ives in the Office of the Librarian of Congress at Washington

125 NASSAU ST. NEW YORK.

WINTER SPORTS – PICKEREL FISHING.

AMERICAN HOMESTEAD WINTER

Meanwhile we did our nightly chores,—
Brought in the wood from out of doors,
Littered the stalls, and from the mows
Raked down the herd's-grass for the cows;
Heard the horse whinnying for his corn;
And, sharply clashing horn on horn,
Impatient down the stanchion rows
The cattle shake their walnut bows;
While, peering from his early perch
Upon the scaffold's pole of birch,
The cock his crested helmet bent
And down his querulous challenge sent.

Unwarmed by any sunset light
The gray day darkened into night,
A night made hoary with the swarm
And whirl-dance of the blinding storm,
As zig-zag, wavering to and fro,
Crossed and recrossed the winged snow:
And ere the early bedtime came
The white drift piled the window-frame,
And through the glass the clothes-line posts
Looked in like tall and sheeted ghosts.

Snow-Bound, A Winter Idyll by John Greenleaf Whittier, 1866

AMERICAN HOMESTEAD
WINTER
1868

This charming scene of rural life in the country is one of a set of four, the others showing American homestead life in the other three seasons. It was the most popular set ever issued by Currier & Ives and a fine example of Nathaniel Currier's practice of issuing series. (His most ambitious set was the so-called *Darktown Comics*, a somewhat disparaging view of Negro life which at the time was considered humorous. This series numbered one hundred in all, and was snapped up by Britain's Duke of Newcastle one day when he happened to be passing the store. Seventy-three thousand were sold of one print in this set, the biggest single sale of a Currier & Ives print which has come to light.) Ives was an adept writer of titles, and he used some words over and over when they proved to sell well. According to a count recently made by the Currier & Ives expert Colin Simkin, the word "American" appears under more than two hundred prints; "great" more than ninety times; "grand" seventy times; and "celebrated," seventy. Other stand-bys were "champion," "splendid," and, of course, "home." "Winter," as evidenced in the present volume, was another sure-fire word —five are included in these pages.

AMERICAN HOMESTEAD WINTER.

SPILL-OUT ON THE SNOW

There were nine teams altogether; our places had been assigned by lot. It was settled that any one who could pass another without danger might do so; but a collision was to involve the hindmost of the two sleighs in the disgrace of taking the last place in the procession. . . . Number four was the doctor's sleigh, with Nellie and her friend. . . . I made up my mind, so insanely excited had I become, that I would pass the doctor at the first turn we came to, no matter what the consequences to life or limb. But I was foiled. At the first corner, I shouted to him to make way, and flourished my long whip over the horses; but he shrewdly planted his sleigh squarely in the middle of the road, and rendered it quite impossible to pass him. My turn was coming, however. We came to a place where the road skirts the mountain in a regular curve for three quarters of a mile, with a steady descent throughout the whole distance. Of course the advantage of "the inside track" on such a breakneck race as we were running was quite apparent. My neighbor saw it, and drove as close to the mountainside as his horses would go. I watched him. At a spot where the road descended suddenly for a few paces, I suddenly shouted, "Make way inside!"—dashed my team almost between him and the hill-side, and drew them back suddenly. The ruse succeeded. With a tremendous effort he forced his horses off the track into the snow nearest the hill and, as was to be expected, upset his sleigh and tossed his ladies into the snow; at which moment I passed, shouting lustily and crowing, with my team snorting proudly at the feat.

"Our Sleigh-Ride," *Harper's Weekly*, February 27, 1858

SPILL-OUT ON THE SNOW
1870

A century ago, if he had the means, a man had a horse instead of an automobile, but even then it was important how fast he could go. When roads began to be extensively developed, particularly in the Northeast, the appearance of two or more rigs on the road was a signal for a race, and more elaborate trials were organized regularly, like the one at right with nine sleighs involved. The American standardbred horse proved to be a superb trotter, and, while racing was frowned upon by the clergy, trotting with a sulky or a sleigh was highly respectable. Broadway, in New York City, was taken over by sleighs during snowy seasons; box-like carts, designed for twenty people but sometimes carrying up to eighty, were a common sight in the seventies. (A drawing by Winslow Homer in the *Harper's Weekly* of January 14, 1860, shows a "spill-out" on Broadway.) This print, unsigned, was probably at least partially the work of Louis Maurer, who also did *Trotting Cracks on the Snow*, another Currier & Ives lithograph to be found in this collection. Or it may have been the work of Thomas Worth, whose custom it was to go to the track and sketch from life. Maurer, who had studied the anatomy of the horse in his native Germany, was the horse expert in the firm, but many of the regulars also did horses. He joined Nathaniel Currier in 1852 at a salary of $5 a week and left eight years later because he wanted $25 a week to get married. He had to look for it at another firm. His relationship with Currier & Ives remained friendly, however, and he did much work afterward for them

ENTERED ACCORDING TO ACT OF CONGRESS IN THE YEAR 18— BY CURRIER & IVES IN THE CLERKS OFFICE OF THE DISTRICT COURT OF THE UNITED STATES FOR THE SOUTHERN DISTRICT OF NEW YORK.

"A SPILL OUT" ON THE SNOW.

NEW YORK PUBLISHED BY CURRIER & IVES 115 NASSAU STREET

WINTER IN THE COUNTRY: GETTING ICE

While yet it is cold in January, and snow and ice are thick and solid, the prudent landlord comes from the village to get ice to cool his summer drink; impressively, even pathetically wise, to foresee the heat and thirst of July now in January—wearing a thick coat and mittens! when so many things are not provided for. It may be that he lays up no treasures in this world which will cool his summer drink in the next. He cuts and saws the solid pond, unroofs the house of fishes, and carts off their very element and air, held fast by chains and stakes like corded wood, through the favoring winter air, to wintry cellars, to underlie the summer there. It looks like solidified azure, as, far off, it is drawn through the streets. These ice-cutters are a merry race, full of jest and sport, and when I went among them they were wont to invite me to saw pit-fashion with them, I standing underneath. . . . Ice is an interesting subject for contemplation. They told me that they had some in the ice-houses at Fresh Pond five years old which was as good as ever. Why is it that a bucket of water soon becomes putrid, but frozen remains sweet forever? It is commonly said that this is the difference between the affections and the intellect.

Walden by Henry David Thoreau, 1854

WINTER IN THE COUNTRY:
GETTING ICE
1864

Both Currier and Ives believed firmly in supplying the public with "popular" prints at cheap prices, as their flyers said, and they succeeded admirably in serving the popular taste. But they were also equally determined to provide value for money: that is, works of quality by distinguished artists, particularly in the production of their large folios. Among the artists they commissioned at various times were Eastman Johnson, Charles Parsons, George Catlin, Thomas Worth, Thomas Nast, Arthur Fitzwilliam Tait, and George Henry Durrie. Durrie, who specialized in scenes of New England winter, painted some of the most famous Currier & Ives prints, such as *Home to Thanksgiving*. This Durrie scene, somewhat lesser known, is equally fine. His landscapes were often as bleak and forbidding as New England winters themselves: *Winter Morning: Feeding the Chickens* or *The Old Grist Mill* are distinctly chilly in feeling. But *Getting Ice*, with its skaters in the background and a dog sprawled happily on the ice in the foreground, is warm as well as icy. Durrie himself was something of the same—a God-fearing New Haven worthy who sang resonantly in the choir, but never entered his studio on a Sunday for fear he might pick up a brush. He provided paintings for no more than a dozen Currier & Ives prints, but they were clearly of his own stamp, done with conscientious attention to detail, every lichen, snowbank and bare tree carefully limned. The lovely print opposite is now quite rare, although fifty years ago it was commonplace.

WINTER IN THE COUNTRY.

Getting Ice.

AMERICAN RAILROAD SCENE: SNOWBOUND

Back in 1856, when I was running between Chicago and Waukegan, a furious storm buried our tracks twenty feet in places. However, we did not wish to abandon the runs, and at the usual hour I started out for Chicago with my train. . . . There was about a mile of clear track for the engine to start on, and when it came flying down the level for its first bout with the snow, our superintendent, Colonel Johnson, jumped on a fence, in his excitement, "to see the fun." I warned him he was too close for safety, but he laughed at the idea of danger, and there he stayed, while I hastened to the center of a big field. A moment later the engine went into the snow bank with a rush, and almost at the same moment Mr. Johnson went off the fence in a back somersault, landing in a drift ten feet away. He had been struck by a section of the snow dashed aside by the engine, but fortunately was not hurt. The engine could make no progress against that enormous bulk of snow, and nearly two hundred men were set to work shoveling it off the track. For over a week not a train passed over the road.

Forty Years on the Rail, Reminiscences of a Veteran Conductor,
by Charles B. George, 1887

AMERICAN RAILROAD SCENE: SNOWBOUND
1871

The building of American railroads was quite properly regarded by the Americans of the day as a great epic story: there was no thought of pollution or energy crises or the destruction of bucolic pleasures, except on the part of a maverick like Henry David Thoreau. As Robert Louis Stevenson ecstatically observed, writing in *Across the Plains* about the completion of the transcontinental railroad, "If it be romance, if it is contrast, if it be heroism that we require, what was Troy to this?" The railroads certainly did require herculean feats on the part of the builders, the laborers, financiers, and, indeed, the passengers. Although the shovellers in the picture opposite were evidently part of a crew, it was not at all unusual for the passengers to get the snow off the track when the need arose. It was also not uncommon for a brakeman or an engineer to wade over to a farmhouse for food, and more than one conductor rode on the bumper of the engine, holding a shovel down on the rail to clean the track. The railroad prints by Currier & Ives number only about thirty of the more than seven thousand issued by the firm, but they have always been among the most popular. Billowing black smoke and steam and glaring lights were also considered to add to the picture: they were clear evidence of man's triumph over the elements.

PUBLISHED BY CURRIER & IVES   ENTERED ACCORDING TO ACT OF CONGRESS IN THE YEAR 1871 BY CURRIER & IVES IN THE OFFICE OF THE LIBRARIAN OF CONGRESS AT WASHINGTON   152 NASSAU ST NEW YORK

AMERICAN RAILROAD SCENE.
SNOW BOUND

SNOWED UP:
RUFFED GROUSE IN WINTER

A *magnificent* bird, the blue or dusky grouse, is found all through the main forest belt, though not in great numbers. They like best the heaviest silver fir woods near garden and meadow openings, where there is but little underbrush to cover the approach of enemies. When a flock of these brave birds, sauntering and feeding on the sunny, flowerly levels of some hidden meadow or Yosemite valley far back in the heart of the mountains, sees a man for the first time in their lives, they rise with hurried notes of surprise and excitement and alight on the lowest branches of the trees, wondering what the wanderer may be, and showing great eagerness to get a good view of the strange vertical animal. Knowing nothing of guns, they allow you to approach within a half-dozen paces, then quietly hop a few branches higher or fly to the next tree without a thought of concealment, so that you may observe them as long as you like, near enough to see the fine shading of their plumage, the feathers on their toes, and the innocent wonderment in their beautiful wild eyes.

Our National Parks by John Muir, 1901

SNOWED UP:
RUFFED GROUSE IN WINTER
1867

This lithograph, one of the most sought after today of the Currier & Ives inventory and as usual unsigned, has been variously attributed to Arthur Fitzwilliam Tait and, recently, to Fanny Palmer. Either could have done it: they both did very similar studies of wild game. Tait, whose only specialty was outdoor prints, was born in England and studied art at the Royal Institute in Manchester. Arriving in the United States in 1851, he became a full member of the National Academy of Design within eight years. Unlike other Currier & Ives regulars, particularly Fanny Palmer, he was often a thorny fellow to deal with. He complained in his letters about the quality of the reproduction of his paintings; he objected to giving the lithographer equal billing on the face of the print, even if he were an artist of note, like Charles Parsons. And he complained that details of his paintings had been lost in the transfer to stone. Currier and Ives treated him with care. They engaged outside artists, often too good for the work and simply out of funds, to color his work, instead of using the corps of German girls in the factory. To secure the services of such a man as Parsons, they even agreed occasionally to have the print manufactured by another firm for which Parsons worked at the time. Unlike the prints of other artists, Tait's work has been consistently admired since it first appeared. His reputation, like Fanny Palmer's, did not die to be born again in the twenties: he has been a major figure for a hundred years.

PUBLISHED BY CURRIER & IVES.

Entered according to Act of Congress AD 1867, by Currier & Ives, in the Clerk's Office of the District Court of the United States, for the Southern District of N.Y.

SNOWED UP:
RUFFED GROUSE IN WINTER

A RIDE TO SCHOOL

But the greatest charm that Winter brought with it was the Christmas holidays. The knowledge that, for six weeks, we should be freed from the trammels of school, neither pestered with grammar, history, geography, round nor text hand—this was indeed, something like a pleasure to look forward to; to know that we should revel among all kinds of games and merry makings; and feed on mince-pies, and sausages, and spareribs, and turkeys and roast geese. . . . Then what pleasure it afforded us to see the preparations which were made for keeping Christmas! the armfuls of holly, and ivy, and mistletoe, which men, women, and boys went by with, as they returned from the woods! But the greatest of all delights was to assist in decorating our own house with those evergreens; to get upon a chair, and stick a sprig of holly here, and a sprig of ivy there, around the pictures, and around the mirror, and above the book-case; over the door, and over the mantel-piece; and around the portrait of some old ancestor, whose smile had lighted up many a merry Christmas in former days. . . . And, in the centre of the large room, there hung the mistle-toe-bough, under which all who were caught there were compelled to pay the same forfeit: and rare fun was there, when the grave old grandmother was caught as she passed under the mistletoe; and honest-hearted grand-dad jumped up to give the dear old lady a kiss. Ah! there was a deal of hearty humour in those days, although the manners of our forefathers were much ruder than those of our own time.

The Boys' Winter Book by Thomas Miller, 1847

A RIDE TO SCHOOL
1872-1874

Children in Currier & Ives prints, for the most part, were drawn as little adult sobersides, a common practice in the moralistic art of the nineteenth century. But the children in this print are distinctly juvenile in aspect, and having a good time. The print is undated and unsigned, but its date can be approximated. It was one of Currier & Ive's most disposable items, probably sold on a table outside the shop for anything down to a nickel, and intended to be mounted on a fire screen or a tavern wall. It was designed to be thrown away when it got torn, and the idea was, of course, that you would buy another to replace it. Nevertheless, even a print like this displays the Currier & Ives warmth and charm. Children, of course, were always a happy subject, and they have always enjoyed the snow. But they do not always proceed so blithely to school as the trio on the opposite page; they are generally more light-hearted on the way back. In the Victorian age, however, which the Currier & Ives period most certainly was, children liked what was good for them, and so they trudged happily to school.

PUBLISHED BY CURRIER & IVES 125 NASSAU ST. NEW YORK

A RIDE TO SCHOOL.